Phillips of Shiptonthorpe

School bus operators in the Yorkshire Wolds area

by Stuart Emmett and John Briggs

A description of the area served by Phillips

The area covered by Phillips was mainly in the East Riding of Yorkshire, a county divided into three shares called Ridings. This all changed in 1974 when the North Yorkshire and Humberside Districts replaced the East Riding.

Phillips were based in Shiptonthorpe, around 5 miles from Pocklington and 2 miles from Market Weighton. Pocklington, with a population of about 8,000, 12 ½ miles east of York and 22 miles northwest of Hull, is at the foot of, and the gateway to, Yorkshire Wolds in East Yorkshire. The Wolds make an arc from the Humber Estuary west of Hull up to the North Sea coast between Bridlington and Scarborough. Here they rise up to form cliffs, most notably at Flamborough, Bempton and Filey. A national footpath, the Wolds Way passes close to Pocklington at Millington in the central Wolds.

The Wolds comprises many low hills and steep valleys underlain by chalk. This unusual topography results in an "upside-down" farming system with livestock (mostly sheep and cows) grazing in the valleys, and the hills above being used for crops. Most of the valleys are therefore in open space and are not former river valleys; indeed surface water is rare in the Wolds. However, southwest of Pocklington towards Selby runs the River Derwent that rises in the North Yorkshire National Park on Fylingdales Moor, near to the coastal town of Scarborough. It runs for around 100 miles through the Vale of Pickering, passing Pickering, Malton, and Stamford Bridge to the east of York, then south through the flat and arable lands to the southwest of Pocklington, meandering across its flood plain and passing several scattered villages amongst open fields in the Vale of York. This area lies west of the undulating foothills of the Yorkshire Wolds with the 10 mile long Pocklington Canal joining the Derwent at East Cottingwith. From there the River Derwent goes down to drain into the River Ouse near to Barmby on the Marsh.

© Stuart Emmett and John Briggs, 2023.

First published in the United Kingdom, 2023,
by Stenlake Publishing Ltd.,
54-58 Mill Square,
Catrine, Ayrshire,
KA5 6RD

Telephone: 01290 551122
www.stenlake.co.uk

ISBN 9781840339642

Printed by P2D,
1 Newlands Road,
Westoning,
MK45 5LD

The publishers regret that they cannot supply copies of any pictures featured in this book.

References

The Independent Coach Operators of the Yorkshire Traffic Area, Part 1, June 1971, PSV Circle and Omnibus Society.

'Lifting the lid off the Cuckoo's Nest', article in *Vintage Roadscene* magazine dated February 2010.

York Independents-Eastern Stage Bus Operators, Stuart Emmett, 2020.

Authors' Note

We hope you enjoy this book. It has been pleasurable to research and write and would not have happened without the many wonderful photographers of the past. We are grateful to them all, for their foresight, and for sharing their images. John Briggs took many pictures of Phillips buses at work and has made an invaluable contribution to this book. Static buses in the depot/yard and various laybys/car parks would merely reflect the hundreds of pictures available from dealers and on the internet, whereas John's pictures are mainly of Phillips buses on the move. This book largely showcases John's work.

Other image providers are John Bennett, Mike Davies and John Sinclair who have also been helpful with further details of this enigmatic operator. We thank them for their assistance along with John Brown, Peter Blanchard and Andrew Sefton who helped with their direct experience of school bus transport. The division of labour of this joint book is Stuart with approx. 80% of the words and 20% of the images, and John with 80% of the images and 20% of the words. The proceeds from the book sales, after deduction of costs, are going 100% to assist on bus preservation and maintaining archives. Indeed, some of the image suppliers and photographers have also donated their images to support this initiative.

Schooling

Like elsewhere, children in the Wolds area initially attended local infant and primary schools. The school experience then became more centralised at the next, secondary school level. The compulsory 11 plus examination, introduced in 1944, graded children between grammar schools and what became known as comprehensive schools, which covered children in the 11-16 years old group and had a larger catchment area.

Most children got to/from school by bus arranged by the local authorities. However, local authority policy was variable. For example, not every local authority put school bus contracts out to tender yearly.

The opening dates of the newly-built comprehensive schools was varied. Pocklington Woldgate School opened in 1957, Barlby near Selby in 1960, Fulford York in 1963, Howden 1963 and Driffield in 1964. Where comprehensive schools were late in building, those scholars scheduled for that school would usually stay at the village schools longer, whilst those that passed the 11 plus went to the existing grammar schools at age 11.

As secondary school transport for pupils more than three miles from the school was free, school bus provision changed with the opening of the new and differently located comprehensive schools. At Pocklington for example Phillips bought nine Leyland Beadles (fleet numbers 11 to 19) in 1958; and in 1960 they bought one Bedford OWB, two SBs and six OBs (fleet numbers 23 to 31); the dates being concurrent with full opening of the comprehensive schools at Pocklington and Barlby.

Nine of these Leyland Beadles came to Phillips from Lincolnshire RCC in 1958. New in 1948/49 they were an integral build by Beadle using former pre-war Leyland buses for parts. They served Phillips until the mid-1960s.

Stuart Emmett Collection

Phillips School buses

Clive Harry Chorley Phillips was born in Pocklington in August 1921. On leaving school, he possibly helped his father, Dick, with his fish and fruit business, although a census record shows Clive was a labourer for a slater. The family moved to Hull Road, Shiptonthorpe in 1939, then the Second World War came. There is no record of Clive's war service (not unusual). After he was demobbed, in September 1952 the school bus business was started at premises on either side of Clay Lane, situated off the Market Weighton to Shiptonthorpe road. Clive was living at Brookfield, Clay Lane, Shiptonthorpe.

Phillips started with just two second-hand buses and the early fleet was as follows:

- 1952: two buses (Bedford OB & OWB)
- 1953: four buses (plus a Bedford WTB and an OWB)
- 1957: seven buses (plus a Bedford OWB, Commer, Guy and Bedford OB)
- 1960: 26 buses (more Bedford OBs, along with many Leyland Beadles and a Bedford SB)

Phillips could reinstate former buses thought to have been withdrawn and some buses purchased were never operated, so the fleet size is indicative only.

Phillips eventually gained a large share of the available school bus work, with some saying they got this by tendering a low price and then just before starting, threatening to pull out unless they got more money. Such comments may be just a result of "sour grapes" from those who were left out, as over time this would be an unsustainable practice.

By early 1971 the fleet had grown to 42 buses and the buses were to say the least, variable. No buses were ever bought new and instead came from many other operations, including military and government sources, with at least 21 such vehicles being re-registered between 1952 and 1971. Up to 1971, Bedfords were a main buy (WTB/OWB/OB/SB/SBG/SBO, SB3/8) followed by Commer Avengers (I/II/III/IV) along with the rare buys like Guy, Sentinel, Austin, and Leyland-Beadle.

The main sources of buses were independents plus the larger Tilling and BET companies, for example Lincolnshire RCC (nine) Northern General (five) with also Western Welsh, Western National and Wilts & Dorset and others providing a few buses each. All were single deckers except two AEC Regent double deckers originating with Glasgow CT and one double decker from Trent. These double deckers were never seen in service and came from Hawker Siddeley at Brough in 1965. Possibly Phillips did a deal to supply buses for staff transport and also acquired their buses.

As the years progressed, council boundary reorganisations and economic realities meant that Phillips slowly lost their monopoly position.

The depot

On the right of Clay Lane was the workshop, complete with a pair of under cover hydraulic lifts. At the rear of this building a corrugated lean-to structure was built between 1975 and 1980, today occupied by a dealer selling ex-military vehicles, especially Land Rovers.

The right side of depot in September 1980 with the imposing office block complex and the workshop behind. **John Briggs**

August 1988 with ex-East Midlands 1960 Leyland Tiger Cub/MCW DP41F. Behind is the depot entrance and field with, alongside, an abandoned small bus in the former grey livery.
John Bennett

The abandoned bus was LYH 285, a Morris with Jones B17F body new in 1951 and with Phillips in September 1965. It came from nearby Full Sutton, the former air force station from 1944 to 1963. This site still has a small landing strip for light aircraft and also houses an industrial estate and a maximum security prison.

LYH was withdrawn by Phillips in November 1968 and photographed there on the 28th June 1987 where it kept "guard" by the entrance to the field for many years.

Mike Davies

The left side of the depot in September 1980. **John Briggs**

On the left of Clay Lane was an older garage, which looked like a 1930s petrol station with petrol pumps. This is now Brookfield Business Park with blocks of newly-built small offices/premises.

Ex-Reading NDP 426 and sister 423 were new to Reading Corporation in September 1957, AEC Reliances with Burlingham B34D plus 35 standee bodywork. Seen in August 1978, it is still in Reading livery. **John Bennett**

Buses were regularly delicensed, especially during the summer school holidays whilst others were bought purely for spares; Phillips was a low-cost operation who clearly kept a close control on expenditure. They also had a large site that presented a "large company" image, as did their eventual red/white bus livery; behind this presentation however, there was for some people, another view.

Phillips very rarely sold withdrawn vehicles and instead parked them in fields behind the premises on either side of Clay Lane. Most of them remained there even after operations finished in 1988. Fortuitously, Mike Davies took the following pictures in 1975 of the main field.

These wonderful pictures make you drool at the treasure trove that was slowly rusting away. **Mike Davies**

John Briggs also took similar pictures in May 1980 and for comparison they are shown here, the growth of the vegetation over 5 years is also noticeable as is the rear extension to the front "office" building.

John Briggs

ROH 200 was acquired in November 1968 and is seen here in April 1986. A Leyland Tiger Cub with Duple Elizabethan coach body that never ran in service or recorded with Phillips, but presumably was bought for parts. **Mike Davies**

Seeing and visiting the buses in the field/depot was not easy it seems. One enthusiast had visited several times with a friend and on one occasion his friend was chased off by the owner who was waving a shotgun. Whilst Mr. Phillips was reported by many as not being friendly to bus enthusiasts, some others did get access and also learned that access was later restricted due to the theft of parts. It was reported that weekends were the best days to attend as no operations took place on those days from the depot; conversely it is also reported, that at weekends, Mr. Phillips said his time was, as he put it, his own.

Another comment on the Old Buses Website notes that Mr. Phillips' view was that since he was demobbed, he had worked hard to build the business up, using vehicles nearing the end of their life. He said it was hard going with such an old fleet to maintain and the interference of bus spotters was never to be allowed. Additionally, also noted by someone who bought a bus to be preserved was, *"In my dealings with him he was fair and took me all round the two fields telling me the stories of every bus he had from his favourite Roe Dalesman and his first wooden seated OWB onwards. He did say the day he closed he would open the place to spotters but of course this never happened as the company was taken over and closed"*.

School bus operations

By the nature of the work, buses did not rack up many miles as they worked a morning and evening return 5 days a week and also had many weeks of no work during weekends and school holidays. Furthermore, many buses "stayed away" on school days and could be found parked in the local countryside near to schools during the day. At night they were often to be found near the homes of their drivers or at other small bases (such as public car parks, pub car parks, laybys etc). It can be noted that licensed operator premises were not required at this time for "the place where vehicles were normally parked".

As the operation grew, the following locations have been identified where buses were parked:

- In the west: York, Pocklington, Barlby (and also mentioned is Harlthorpe)
- In the south: Howden rail station, Eastrington (also mentioned are Gilberdyke, and Balkholme near Howden)
- In the north: Norton near Malton (however, no pictures have been seen of buses in this area)
- In the east: Kirkburn near Driffield (also mentioned are Beverley, Halsham near Withernsea and Filey, but again, no picture confirmation has been seen)

It has been noted that many buses, increasingly in the late 1970s, were in poor condition and it has been said that if such vehicles were to turn up for school runs today, there would be an outcry. The poor condition of buses is reflected by one report of buses with holes in the floor down which the school children were dangling school satchels. This caused complaints and indeed in at least once instance, to Phillips losing contracts. The fleet, however, was "smartened up" in the decade before the 1988 closure and John Briggs' memories of Phillips buses from the late 1970s are that they always looked smart.

The bus livery was two tone grey, then perhaps experimentally, at least two buses were lined out in red as were the wheel hubs (as seen later on DCN 910 photographed in 1972 and WWF 496J in 1978). Perhaps these were the only two so painted, as around the mid 1970s a red/white livery was adopted; coincidentally buses bought were often red and operated sometimes with the previous owners name painted over.

Showing the former PMT name painted over, is 735 CVT from the batch 731 to 745. At Howden Station in March 1972 is this 1957 Albion Aberdonian with Weymann B44F body, one of several that came to Phillips from Potteries MT, including the later ones 748/58/60. These, however, had Willowbrook bodies and were from the batch 746 to 760. **John Bennett**

Drivers could come from Phillips central pool. The pattern seemed to be that in the early days of running a contract, it would be served from Shiptonthorpe, whilst a search for local drivers along the route was made. The preferred option for a low cost operation was for a school teacher to be the bus driver, although other local people were trained such as publicans, retired people, and stay-at-home parents.

Buses at work

It has not been possible to definitively identify all the Phillips routes between 1952 and 1988 as Philips chose to not register them. However, full details of the current school services are readily available and with the assumption that there has been little change from the routes in the Phillips years, these current school service routes have been used to give a more structured guide to view the Phillips buses at work.

The following map may also be of assistance in locating the routes:

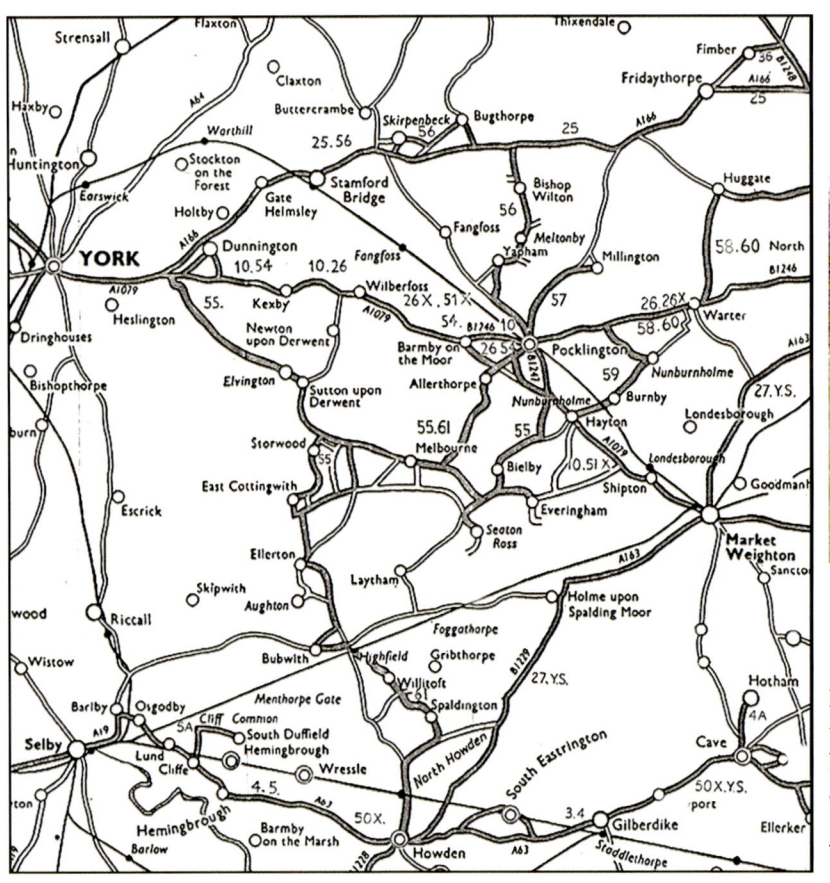

PCW 956.
John Briggs

Phillips had from late 1979, what could be said to be their "standard bus"; these being the thirteen Leyland Tiger Cub PSUC1/eleven with East Lancs B43F bodies that came from Burnley, Colne, and Nelson (latterly Burnley & Pendle).

This 1954 map shows the East Yorkshire stage bus routes in the area.

The Tiger Cubs came from four batches and were new between 1963 and 1967; details follow:

- 1963 PCW 956-959, in June 1979 to Phillips and stayed until 1988
- 1964 BCW 463/7B, to Phillips in April 1980, 463 stayed to the end in 1988 but 467 left the fleet in 1985
- 1965 BHG 360-2/4C, to Phillips in April 1980 and all stayed until 1988 with 360 going over to EYMS
- 1967 FHG 570-3C, 570-572 to Phillips in January 1980 and, 573 in February 1980; 570/1/3 stayed until the end in 1988 but 572 was withdrawn in 1986. 570 passed over to EYMS

The 1980 intake was large, and whether these were normal fleet replacement, or for new contracts, is not currently known. Some initially ran in their BCN livery before later getting the normal Phillips red livery.

A popular place for enthusiasts to watch Phillips buses was by their depot in the afternoon when four to six buses left between 1500 and 1530 hours for school pick-ups. A small selection of the buses seen at this location follows.

With the driver "doffing his cap" on the 12th September 1980, AEK 514 came from Wigan CT and was a Leyland PSU1/13 with Northern Counties body new in 1953. It survived Phillips and was preserved, as was its sister AEK 516 which was also with Phillips. **John Briggs**

With the friendly driver again, FHG 571C was a 1967 Leyland Tiger Cub with East Lancs body from Burnley Colne & Nelson (BCN) heading towards the A1079 on 26th June 1981. On the left is part of the depot and the bungalow, named "Brookfield" that was the first home on this site of Clive Phillips.

John Briggs

DAX 604C on 19th March 1982 was a 1965 Bristol MW from Red & White, latterly National Welsh. Sisters DAX 609 and 612C were also with Phillips in November 1978. In the middle left background over the parked bus is a house roof; this was the new home of Clive Phillips called "Brooklands" and was beyond the office complex on the right side of Clay Lane.

John Briggs

From York Fulford school

Ex-Potteries Albion/Willowbrook 758 CVT near to Fulford school, York in March 1972. **John Bennett**

In July 1978 is WWF 496J showing the normal two shades of the grey livery with the lighter shade as a wide stripe, and with unusual and perhaps experimental red wheels that match the red lining. A former military Bedford approaching Fulford School in York with I assume, mum driving and daughter alongside. **John Bennett**

Earlier in October 1972 with DCN 910 seems to have been another experiment using a darker version of the two tone grey livery, along with red wheels and red lining. At St. Johns College in York it was one of five former Northern AEC/Park Royal Monocoach integrals bought in late 1969/early 1970 (the others were DCN 906, 908, 915, 919). DCN 910 was later painted in the red livery and eventually went for preservation after being with Phillips. **John Bennett**

A 1960 AEC Reliance with Harrington Cavalier C37F body new to Timpson's in London, XXT511 then passed to Margo's, Streatham in 1969. It was withdrawn in November 1971, sold on to Davis in Grafham, Hunts in June 1972 and to Phillips (along with XXF 514) in February 1973 and withdrawn in 1978. Seen here in June 1974 XXT 511 is approaching Fulford School in York. **John Bennett**

From Barlby, near Selby

In Barlby, Selby on 12th June 1980 is WAJ 796, a Ford Thames Trader 570E with Duple Yeoman C41F body, which was new in 1960 to Watson, based at Huntington in York. Phillips worked for the secondary school in Barlby from its opening in 1960 and initially had three routes operated by Bedford OBs. Other operators had another three routes, one of which was Gorwood of East Cottingwith (and covered in *York Independents-Eastern Stage Bus Operators,* Stuart Emmett, 2020). **John Briggs**

From Garton near Driffield

On 5th October 1981 leaving a small primary school in Garton on the Wolds, about three miles from Driffield, is a former BCN Tiger Cub. It has arrived and waited ten minutes by the small primary school close to the large tree and is now heading off towards Kirkburn, four miles away on the A614.
John Briggs

17th July 1984 and back at Garton on the Wolds with the grass cut and the sign now partly missing. 324 EDV, an ex-Western National Bristol SUL with ECW B36F body was new to Southern National in 1961. Withdrawn in March 1972 and passed to Primrose Valley, Hunmanby but only stayed two months and went to a contractor in Driffield in May 1972. It was with Phillips by 1981 and worked until around June 1986, and was sold to Ripley, Carlton in April 1989. **John Briggs**

September 1979 with Garton Church tower in the background 862 RAE is heading for Kirkburn, where it slept overnight. A 1962 Bristol SUS/ECW B30F from Bristol OC via Primrose Valley Coaches of Hunmanby near Filey it was with Phillips from 1974 to around 1983 and then passed to a dealer in June 1993. It was eventually preserved as Bristol 301. **John Briggs**

Market Weighton to Londesborough

On the 23rd October 1987 on Intake Lane to Londesborough, is JBR 102F, one of three RELL/MCW B50D buses from Tyne & Wear PTE that came to Phillips (JBR 100/2/F). Coincidentally many also went to Burnley and Pendle, the then current name for the former Burnley, Colne & Nelson, and a supplier of many buses to Phillips. Originally a batch of ten supplied to Sunderland CT in 1968 with a B47D body, the central door was later removed and an emergency exit window fitted; this changed the configuration to B50F. All three buses went to East Yorkshire MS in 1988. The footpath sign is for the "Wolds Way", a 79 mile path from the North Sea coast at Filey, to Hessle, near to the Humber Bridge.

John Briggs

JBR 105F with a different/replacement windscreen is climbing Intake Hill for Londesborough on 9th October 1987. The hill runs from the A614 up into the hamlet, situated just under 3 miles from Market Weighton. **John Briggs**

24th June 1988 near Londesborough with AHL 230K which with AHL 232K came to Phillips from West Riding. The size of the posing boy suggests this was a primary school contract! These 1971 Bristol RELL/ECWB53F would both go to EYMS. **John Briggs**

Pocklington to Ellerton via Newton on Derwent, Sutton on Derwent, and Melbourne

Amongst the vegetables near to Newton on Derwent on 11th July 1980 are a former Leyland Tiger Cub from BCN and a Bristol MW from West Yorkshire RCC. Both are likely waiting to go for the afternoon run from Woldgate School, Pocklington. **John Briggs**

On 12th June 1981 on Bull Balk (balk is a ridge or a bank aka a hill), Newton-on-Derwent, ex-West Yorkshire SMG19, 827 BWY was new in May 1963 and withdrawn in December 1973. It was sold to dealers Paul Sykes in Barnsley in August 1975 and came to Phillips in December 1975. Withdrawn by January 1984 it spent time in the field unitil June 1993 when it went to Parton & Allan at the Carlton scrap yards and eventually found a home for preservation with Neil Halliday, Shipley in 2002. **John Briggs**

NGY 575 to 578 were four Leyland Royal Tiger PSU1/14 with very rare Duple B54F bodies (probably in a 3+2 configuration) bought by the Ministry of Supply in 1953 for the Cumberland nuclear site at Windscale, now known as Sellafield. NGY 576 and 577 came to Phillips and both survived until the end in 1988. NGY 576 is seen on the left passing through Melbourne on a Pocklington contract to either East Cottingwith or Ellerton on 11th September 1981. **John Briggs**

PEF 21 was one of five Leyland Leopards with Strachan B45D bodies that inaugurated OMO in West Hartlepool in 1967. PEF 21 was the one that came to Phillips. Seen with Phillips on 12th June 1981, at Melbourne for either East Cottingwith or Ellerton, complete with lady driver, a rare practice at the time. **John Briggs**

Pocklington to East Cottingwith via Allerthorpe, Thornton and Melbourne

FHG 570E on the 4th June 1982 is heading for Thornton possibly from East Cottingwith. A Leyland Tiger Cub with East Lancs body new in 1967, Phillips had many such buses with two going over to EYMS in 1988. **John Briggs**

324 EDV on 16th July 1982 on Walbut Bridge heads from Melbourne over the Pocklington Canal towards Thornton. **John Briggs**

324 EDV is coming back from Thornton 10 minutes after the previous image of it on 16th July 1982. **John Briggs**

NGY 576 is coming from Thornton on 16th July 1982. **John Briggs**

Pocklington to Seaton Ross via Everingham and Bielby

19th March 1982 with ex-Trent VCH 840 in Everingham on the Pocklington to Seaton Ross run. It was a Leyland Tiger Cub with Willowbrook B45F body new in March 1961. VCH 834/8/9 and 841 were also with Phillips and all survived until 1988. **John Briggs**

On 26th June 1981 VCH 840 is at the junction where the road from Beilby meets the Everingham to Seaton Ross Road. Ex-Trent VCH 840 is coming from Seaton Ross for Everingham and Pocklington. **John Briggs**

On 26th June 1981 at the same junction as VCH 840 above, 324 EDV coming from Seaton Ross has turned left for Bielby and Pocklington. **John Briggs**

Pocklington via Fangfoss for Stamford Bridge, or High Catton or Thixendale
(the route in the 1980s may have stopped at Kirby Underdale or Uncleby)

8th May 1981 with NGY 576 between Pocklington and Fangfoss, a road used for three routes from Woldgate School, Pocklington to Thixendale, High Caton and Stamford Bridge. **John Briggs**

Between Pocklington and Fangfoss on 11th July 1980 is BHG 360C, ex-Burnley Colne & Nelson in April 1980 and still in their livery; later it got the red livery before passing to EYMS in 1988. **John Briggs**

Going through Fangfoss on 25th July 1986 is an ex-BCN Leyland heading for Pocklington. **John Briggs**

Pocklington to Full Sutton via Youlthorpe

FHG 570E, another ex-BCN Tiger Cub, coming from Youlthorpe on 23rd October 1981 and heading for the A166. **John Briggs**

BHG 361C from Full Sutton on 11th May 1984 bound for Youlthorpe. **John Briggs**

11th May 1984 again with BHG 361C turning for Youlthorpe. **John Briggs**

11th May 1984 again with BHG 361C returning from Youlthorpe and about to turn left for Pocklington. **John Briggs**

Pocklington to Thixendale via Yapham, Skirpenbeck, Bugthorpe, Kirby Underdale and Uncleby

One of the Leyland/East Lancs from BCN seen on 25th May 1984 coming back from Thixendale and leaving Kirkby Underdale bound for Bugthorpe.
John Briggs

Ex-BCN PCW 958 is climbing Uncleby Hill near to Kirkby Underdale on 6th July 1984.
John Briggs

Ex-BCN PCW 958 is at the junction at the top of Uncleby Hill near to Kirkby Underdale on 23rd September 1983.
John Briggs

30th April 1982 with PCW 958 near to Kirby Underdale on the Thixendale route. **John Briggs**

PCW 957 on 1st October 1982 had left Bugthorpe and was on the road to Skirpenbeck heading back to Pocklington. **John Briggs**

PCW 957 at Bugthorpe Lane on 17th September 1982.
John Briggs

BHG 360C, seen earlier in BCN livery, is approaching Bugthorpe on Bugthorpe Lane on 3rd October 1986.
John Briggs

An historic image of EYMS LXE 275K on 3rd November 1989 running through Bugthorpe and appropriately heading towards the setting sun as this was the last time a Phillips liveried bus was seen at work by John Briggs.
John Briggs

PCW 957 passes through Skirpenbeck on its way back to Pocklington on 15th October 1982. **John Briggs**

An ex-BCN Tiger Cub seen on 17th May 1987 has left Bugthorpe behind for Skirpenbeck. **John Briggs**

Ex-BCN Leyland/East Lancs on 8th July 1983 near Bugthorpe on the Thixendale route. **John Briggs**

Ex-BCN Leyland/East Lancs on 21st July 1983 near Bugthorpe on the Thixendale route. **John Briggs**

On Bugthorpe Lane returning from Thixendale and near to Bugthorpe. **John Briggs**

PCW 958, another BCN Tiger Cub, on 25th September 1981 at the bottom of Grimthorpe Hill for Great Givendale, Skirpenbeck, Bugthorpe, Kirby Underdale and Thixendale. A tractor to the right has turned onto Swineridge Lane. **John Briggs**

Pocklington to Huggate via Millington and Fridaythorpe

25th September 1981 at the bottom of Grimthorpe Hill with VCH 841, one of the ex-Trent Tiger Cubs, turning right onto Swineridge Lane. It will follow the route to Fridaythorpe and Huggate covered by the next images. **John Briggs**

Another ex-BCN Tiger Cub on 24th July 1981 on Swineridge Lane heading toward Millington for Fridaythorpe and Huggate. Fridaythorpe, at the top of Garrowby Hill on the A166, at 550 feet is the highest village in the Wolds. **John Briggs**

Ex-BCN Tiger Cub on 24th July 1987 turns off Swineridge Lane into Martin Lane for Millington village. **John Briggs**

25th July 1986 at Millington with Bedford VAS/Plaxton C29F TUP 5E new in 1967 to Weardale, Frosterley where it stayed until 1969 then appeared with various East Anglian operators before coming to Phillips. It eventually went to EYMS in 1988 and was recorded in 1990 as being untaxed and possibly had been scrapped. **John Briggs**

On 9th July 1972 ex-Trent VCH 841 has left Millington and is smoking its way up The Balk towards Fridaythorpe and Huggate. **John Briggs**

Climbing The Balk from Millington village in October 1986 is BHG 362C heading for Fridaythorpe and Huggate. **John Briggs**

22nd April 1988 with LXE 275K, a 1972 Bedford SB5 with Plaxton C41F body new to Costin of Dunstable, descending the hill from Fridaythorpe towards Pocklington just before the junction with The Balk to Millington. It went to East Yorkshire in 1988 and was sold in July 1991.
John Briggs

FHG 570E on 25th September 1987 on the hill from Fridaythorpe Road to Pocklington at the junction with The Balk into Millington.
John Briggs

FHG 570E on 19th June 1987 on the Pocklington to Fridaythorpe road just above where The Balk from Millington joins.
John Briggs

Buses at rest

August 1981 during school holidays with many buses parked up: on the left ex-Red & White MW, an ex-Reading AEC Reliance/Burlingham and on the right, an ex-Ribble Leopard with BET style Marshall body. **John Briggs**

Seen on 1st April 1986 at the depot is the Morris Commercial MRA1 one ton 4x4 ex-military truck, along with a former Commer fire engine registered NRH 117 that had been converted into a tow truck. **Mike Davies**

On 18th December 1981 the Morris Commercial truck is leaving the depot to head south to Eastrington and refuel buses out-stationed there. **John Briggs**

Eastrington off the A614 near to Howden on 18th December 1981 with FHG 570E, one of the BCN Tiger Cubs and LCB 55G. This is also a Tiger Cub but with a better-looking East Lancs body that was new to Blackburn CT in July 1969 and another bus that eventually went for preservation after being sold to EYMS in 1988.

This type of vehicle positioning, to minimise avoidable mileage and costs, used to be common practice, particularly among school bus contract operators in rural areas. Tightening of PSV Operator Licensing Regulations, requiring vehicles to be kept at registered Operating Centres, primarily to facilitate spot roadworthiness checks by Government Vehicle Inspectors, subsequently eliminated this practice.
John Briggs

Unusual Buses

Leaving the depot on 19th March 1982 is FRX 162K. With its sister they were new in 1972 to the Atomic Weapons Establishment in Aldermaston and were unique buses. They had Bedford YRQ chassis and Strachan B42D bodies in what could be called, a 1970s utility style! It was also taken on by EYMS. **John Briggs**

NDP 271F was an ex-Reading Bristol RELL with Pennine B34D plus 35 standee type body new in 1968 and built to resemble the early AEC/Burlinghams. Seen on 4th June 1982 parked in the often-used layby near to Gilberdyke, Phillips also had 275/281G. 275G went for preservation. The original Reading standee buses from 1957 used AEC Reliance chassis with Burlingham bodywork and NDP 426 was shown earlier with Phillips. In 1967/68 Reading bought the Bristol RELL chassis and used Strachan to build eleven bodies with Pennine building another 21; both batches were similar. The low floor Bristol chassis enabled deep side windows to give better visibility for standing passengers.
John Briggs

Phillips in preservation. 647 BKL, a Guy Warrior LUF with Meadows engine and Mulliner bodywork was new in 1957 as a non-psv with Leybourne Grange Hospital in Kent and came to Phillips in 1964. Withdrawn in 1969, it was later stored near the left field, on the forecourt between the garage and the bungalow until the early 1990s when, as seen here, it was wonderfully preserved in the two tone grey livery it had when it first entered service with Phillips. It was to be later painted to represent a United AS red liveried bus and was used in the TV series *Heartbeat*. The last report (2018) was of it being for sale on E Bay; its current location and condition is unknown. **Stuart Emmett Collection**

Another Phillips bus in preservation and here returned to its original livery. 966 RVO, is a 1963 Bedford VAL 14 with Yeates body and one of only seven built with dual sliding doors, originally owned by Barton Transport, of Chilwell, Nottingham. It worked for Barton until 1973 when it was sold to Connor & Graham in East Yorkshire, who then sold it on to Phillips in 1975 who used it for three years. It was then left in the field until bought for preservation in November 1984. **By Andrewrabbott – Own work, CC BY-SA 4.0 @ https://commons.wikimedia.org/w/index.php?curid=35362199**

The End

Phillips traded as Phillips Coaches until February 1980, when a limited company, Phillips Coach Company Ltd was formed, but they were not actually a coach company! In June 1988, Mr. Phillips retired aged 67 and sold his company to the East Yorkshire Motor Services group, where it was operated as a subsidiary of the group and in 1989, the company was absorbed into fellow subsidiary, Cherry Coaches Ltd.

EYMS bought 18 vehicles with the other buses, property and land retained by Phillips.

Four of Phillips outside the former East Yorkshire depot at Beverley with an EY double decker. The red shade in the livery is similar on the two Tiger Cubs with East Lancs bodies and the Bedford VAS1/Plaxton. The 18 buses that came to EY from Phillips were seven Bristols (one LH, six REs) four Bedford's (J2, VAS, SB, YRQ) three Leyland Tiger Cubs and 4x7 seaters (BMC J, Rover Sherpa, 2 Bedford CF). **John Sinclair**

Left: 23rd September 1988 outside EYMS, Pocklington is SKB 685G a Bristol RELL/Park Royal B45D new in 1982 to Merseyside PTE. Sister 678G was scrapped by Phillips in August 1988.
John Briggs

Below left: EYMS, Pocklington again on 21st October 1988 with WFE 679M a 1983 Bristol LH/ECW B43F from Lincolnshire.
John Briggs

Below: 21st October 1988 again at EYMS, Pocklington is MUR 209H a Bedford J2 with Plaxton C20F body new as a 15-seater to Rickards, Brentford. It came to Phillips in May 1985 from Beeston, Hadleigh, and went for scrap in July 1992. **John Briggs**

On 10th August 1988 it was noted that the clearance from the premises of the many disused buses had commenced. Phillips sold many buses to varied scrapyards, (such as Johnson's, Wilberfoss, Whiting Brothers, Ferrybridge with many eventually finishing up in the Carleton yards); some also went direct for preservation. The main field on the right of Clay Lane was cleared by 22nd October and the 33 remaining buses were moved to the field on the left to await final disposal. The main yard on the right of Clay Lane, was then occupied by a new tenant (and/or owner) who was an Army surplus vehicle dealer, and are still there today.

18th November 1988 with the right field cleared of buses. Also clearly revealed is the ramp (used mainly for steam cleaning) that was in regular use. Along with other assorted debris, at the back of the field are some ex-military trucks.
John Briggs

The left field on 18th November 1988 after buses have been transferred across the lane.
John Briggs

On 1st January 1991, the following buses were still on the site with a "*" indicating they eventually went for preservation:

Reg. Number	Chassis	Body	New to
FTG 353	Bedford OB	Duple B30F	Jenkins, Skewen
LAM 110*	Bristol LWL	ECW FB39F	Wilts & Dorset
647 BKL*	Guy Warrior	Mulliner B45F	Leybourne Grange Hospital, Kent
AEK 514*/516*	Leyland PSU1/13	NC B43F	Wigan CT
PCW 956/7*/8. BCW 463/467B. BHG 361/362/364C. FHG 573E*.	Leyland PSUC1/1	East Lancs B42F	Burnley, Colne & Nelson (later Burnley and Pendle).
NGY 576/577	Leyland PSU1/14	Duple B54F	Ministry of Supply Windscale/Sellafield
PEF 21*	Leyland L1	Strachan B45D	West Hartlepool
827 BWY*	Bristol MW	ECW B45F	West Yorkshire RCC
TCK 480/483/484. UCK 522.	Leyland PSU3/1R	Marshall B53F	Ribble
NDP 271F/275G*/283G	Bristol RELL	Pennine B34D +35	Reading CT
1252 EV*	Bristol MW	ECW DP41F	Eastern National
VCH 834/838/839/840/841	Leyland PSUC1/1	Willowbrook B45F	Trent
OWX 396K	Bedford YRQ	Willowbrook DP45F	Burley t/a Majestic, Cawood.
862 RAE	Bristol SUS	ECW B30F	Bristol OC

*Note the following buses had already gone for preservation: Leyland Tiger Cub from Edinburgh; VSC 80, Bedford VAL from Barton; 966 RVO, AEC-Park Royal Monocoach from Northern General; DCN 910, Leyland Cub from Blackburn CT; LCB 55G, Bedford OB from Ministry of Works; KXV 562.

Captured on 1st April 1986 is KXV 562 that came to Phillips in March 1958 from the Ministry of Works where it was new in 1950. Delicensed between March 1963 and May 1966, the Bedford OB with reported Mulliner B30F body was withdrawn in May 1968. It spent more time with Phillips in the field than it did working. However, KXV 562 had another short life, as it was bought for preservation in February 1989, but was later scrapped. Alongside is NGY 577, with a tow hook fitted and awaiting its fate. **Mike Davies**

Most buses on site had gone by July 1993 but some lingered; however, in March 2000 only two buses were left that had been used as store sheds, and these were acquired by Carl Ireland, Hull.

The 10th March 2000 and waiting collection are the last two buses on the site. TCK 494 ex-Ribble and PCW 957 ex-Burnley Colne and Nelson. **Mike Davies**

Clive Phillips died a few years later in 2003 aged 82. This was the end of an era that had provided enthusiasts with spectacular variety and, a unique source of buses for preservation.

End Note

Researching Phillips beyond the many images on Flickr and other internet bus sites is problematic, as little other information is available. So, whilst we hope this book partly helps to record some of Phillips, we would be delighted to hear from anyone who has any useful memories or details covering the schools served, reminiscences of the buses, the drivers etc.

Phillips buses were a rich topic and deserve a more complete coverage of the fleet and routes, but this book does give a unique record of many of the buses "at work" from the late 1970s to 1988; indeed many have said that they never saw a moving Phillips bus apart from when seen leaving the depot.